W9-AFZ-585

If your child struggles with a word, you can encourage "sounding it out," but keep in mind that not all words can be sounded out. Your child might pick up clues about a word from the picture, other words in the sentence, or any rhyming patterns. If your child struggles with a word for more than five seconds, it is usually best to simply say the word.

Most of all, remember to praise your child's efforts and keep the reading fun. After you have finished the book, ask a few questions and discuss what you have read together. Rereading this book multiple times may also be helpful for your child.

Try to keep the tips above in mind as you read together, but don't worry about doing everything right. Simply sharing the enjoyment of reading together will increase your child's reading skills and help to start your child off on a lifetime of reading enjoyment!

**About Pets**

A We Both Read® Book

---

*For Maggie, Toto, Squeaky, and Bree—*
*my best friends.*

Text Copyright © 2002 by Sindy McKay
All rights reserved

Use of photographs provided by Getty Images
© copyright 2002

We Both Read™ is a registered trademark of Treasure Bay, Inc.

Published by
Treasure Bay, Inc.
P.O. Box 119
Novato, CA 94948 USA

Printed in Singapore

Library of Congress Catalog Card Number: 2002103855

Hardcover ISBN-13: 978-1-891327-41-4
Paperback ISBN-13: 978-1-891327-42-1

We Both Read® Books
Patent No. 5,957,693

Visit us online at:
www.webothread.com

PR 5-14

WE BOTH READ®

# Parent's Introduction

**Whether your child is a beginning reader, a reluctant reader, or an eager reader, this book offers a fun and easy way to encourage and help your child in reading.**

Developed with reading education specialists, ***We Both Read*** books invite you and your child to take turns reading aloud. You read the left-hand pages of the book, and your child reads the right-hand pages—which have been written at one of six early reading levels. The result is a wonderful new reading experience and faster reading development!

You may find it helpful to read the entire book aloud yourself the first time, then invite your child to participate the second time. As you read, try to make the story come alive by reading with expression. This will help to model good fluency. It will also be helpful to stop at various points to discuss what you are reading. This will help increase your child's understanding of what is being read.

In some books, a few challenging words are introduced in the parent's text, distinguished with **bold** lettering. Pointing out and discussing these words can help to build your child's reading vocabulary. If your child is a beginning reader, it may be helpful to run a finger under the text as each of you reads. Please also notice that a "talking parent" icon precedes the parent's text, and a "talking child" icon precedes the child's text.

WE BOTH READ®

# About Pets

By Sindy McKay

TREASURE BAY

Dogs, cats, fish, birds, lizards, rats—**pets** are everywhere! They come in all different shapes, sizes and colors.

**Pets** can be big.

Pets can be small.

Pets may have lots of **nice** fluffy fur or they may be silky-smooth and shiny. Some pets have scales and some have wings. There are pets with gills and pets with shells.

Can you think of a pet that has a shell?

This is a turtle.

Turtles are **nice** pets.

Different pets have different needs.

Birds need a cage to sleep in, but most cats **sleep** anywhere they want to. A dog must be fed every day, but some snakes only eat once a week.

Good pet owners know what's best for their pet.

Cats like to **sleep** in the sun.

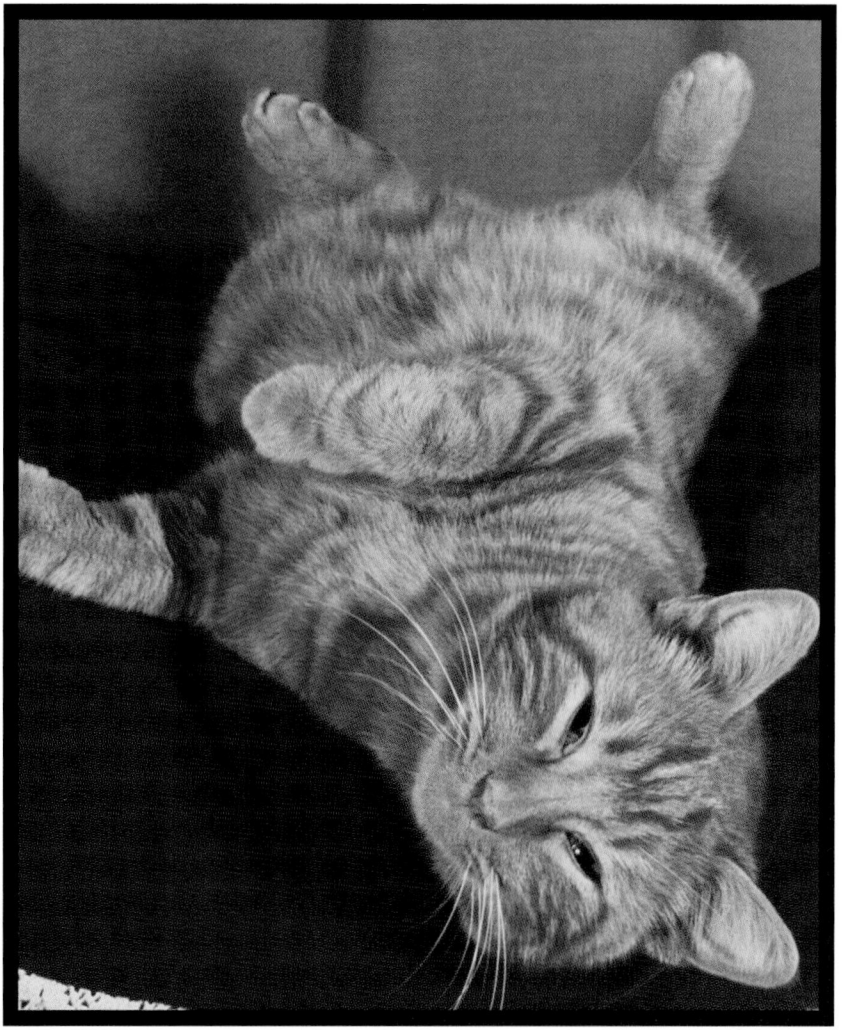

According to some sources, cats are the world's most popular pets. Maybe that's because cats are so easy to care for.

Cats don't seem to mind being left alone while their owners are away at school or work. They can also be very loving and will **purr** contentedly while curled up in your lap.

A cat has soft fur.

It may **purr** if you pet it.

Some people say that dogs are the most popular pets in the world. That could be because there are so many different kinds of dogs to choose from. Or it might just be because a **puppy** is too doggone cute to resist!

A **puppy** is a lot of fun to play with!

Dogs and cats may be the two most common household pets, but there are many other animals that make great pets as well. Some other favorite four-legged friends are rats, hamsters, rabbits, guinea pigs, lizards, turtles, and pigs.

This girl has a big pig for a pet.

Not all pets have four legs. Many people choose birds as pets, while others might choose **fish** or one of several species of snakes.

**Fish** make good pets.
Cats like them, too!

Pet owners try to spend as much time as possible with their pets and many will **talk** to them the same way they **talk** to a good friend.

Birds love to sing.
Some birds can even **talk.**

The variety of pets available is vast and wonderful. But no matter what animal you choose as a pet, it must be well cared for and **loved**.

This dog **loves** to ride in the car.

Owning a pet is a big responsibility. An animal that has become a pet cannot take care of itself. It is the owner's responsibility to provide the right food for their pet along with plenty of fresh water to **drink.**

This is NOT a good way to get a **drink!**

Some pets like to eat the same **food** we eat. However, feeding "people food" to a pet is not a good idea. Pets need to eat special food that has been made just for them.

Some dogs beg for **food.**

Some kids beg for food, too!

Another important aspect of caring for a pet is making sure it gets enough exercise.

Goldfish can take care of getting their own exercise, but cats enjoy playing with toys. Just rolling a ball of yarn across the room can keep a cat busy for a long time.

Dogs love to play.
They love to run and jump.

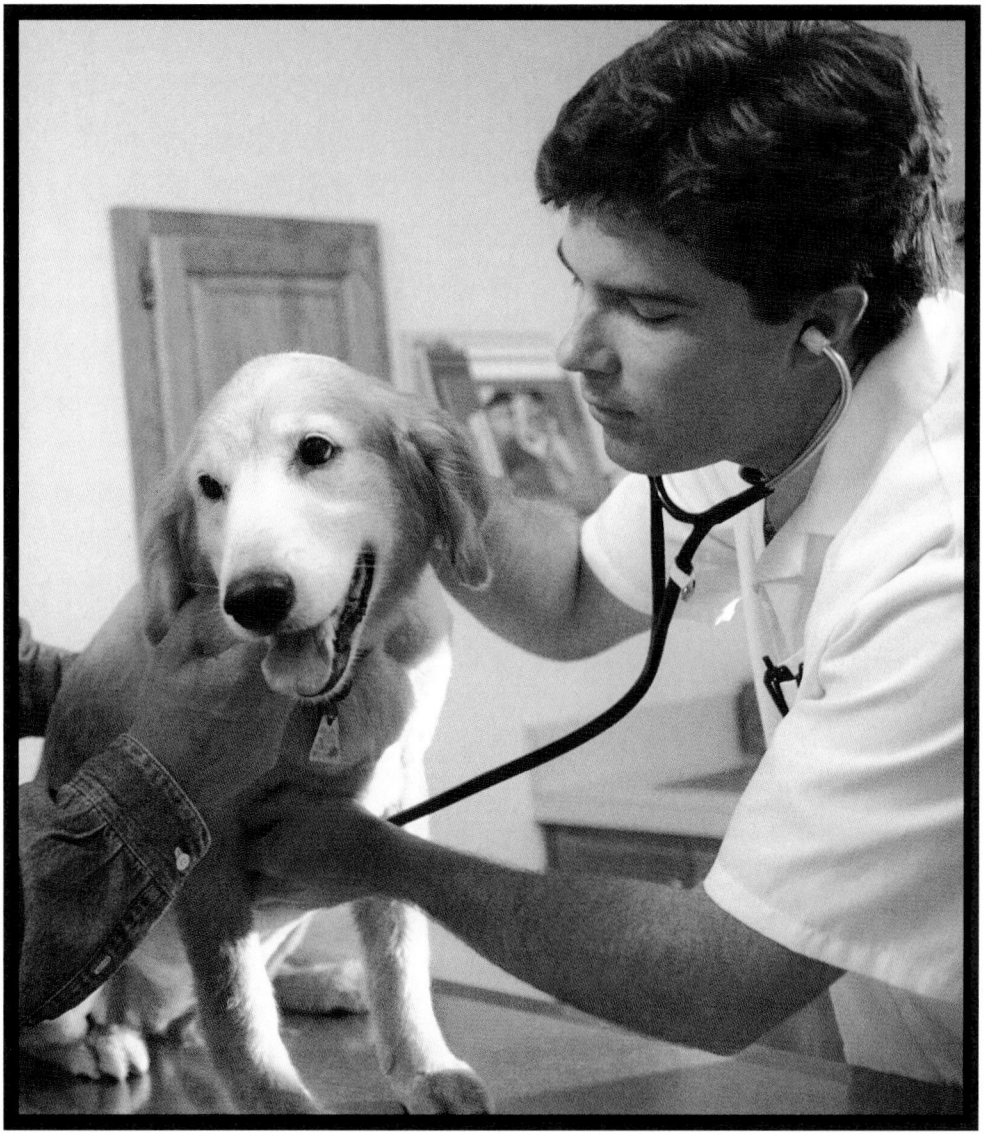

Regular visits to the veterinarian will help assure that your pet stays healthy. A veterinarian can advise you on the right diet and exercise to keep your pet **happy** and give any necessary shots or medicine to prevent disease.

A well pet is a **happy** pet.

Most pets require some kind of bathing and grooming. Many need regular haircuts and **baths,** and some may need to have their nails clipped and their teeth brushed.

Big dogs use big tubs for their **baths**.

Having a place to call home is important for every kind of pet. Birds need a large, clean cage of their very own. Fish **live** in an aquarium. Many reptiles and snakes need a special enclosure with a heater to keep their body temperatures steady.

This dog likes to **live** in the house.

One of the most important things a pet needs to thrive is the time and affection of its owner.

Give your pet a big hug.
It feels good.

If you are thinking of getting a new pet, it's a good idea to spend some time deciding what kind of pet is right for you.

Consider how much time you have to spend with the animal and how much money you are willing to spend on its care and upkeep.

A dog or cat makes
a good pet.

So does a frog.

Few things are **cuter** than a puppy, but a puppy can be a real handful! You might want to think about choosing an older animal that's already been trained.

If you're not going to be home much, consider getting two pets so they can keep each other company.

One dog is cute.

Two dogs are **cuter!**

It doesn't take long for a pet to become part of our lives, and soon we wonder how we ever got along without them.

They join us at work and at **play.** They cheer us up when we're sad and share our joy when we're feeling happy.

They **play** with us.

They even sing with us.

If we give our pets what they need, they will give back to us love and devotion and laughter.

A pet is a very nice thing.

If you liked ***About Pets*** here is another
We Both Read® book you are sure to enjoy!

## About the Seasons

This simple Level 1 book explores the seasons through the changing weather and the changing activities of both children and animals. There is a brief description of why the earth has four seasons, but most of the book is devoted to the delightful new world that each season brings into our life.

To see all the We Both Read books that are available, just go online to **www.WeBothRead.com**.